Dates: _____ to _____

Name: _____

Courses: _____

_____

The End-of-Round Golf Diary

Record detailed notes for 50 rounds of golf

Chris McMullen

The End-of-Round Golf Diary

Copyright (c) 2008 Chris McMullen

All rights reserved. This includes the right to reproduce any portion of this book in any form.

Custom Books

Nonfiction / sports / golf

ISBN: 1438282826

EAN-13: 9781438282824

Using this diary

Complete this diary when you return home from each round of golf. Review your entries periodically to help draw from positive moments in the past and to assess how your game is progressing and areas needing improvement.

The entries are divided into categories to help you see how the course conditions and difficulty affect your score, how well you are performing in various physical and mental aspects of your game, record goals and swing thoughts for each round and assess how they worked, describe memorable shots to draw on for positive visualization in the future, identify which areas of your game to work on, determine your mental strengths and weaknesses, and assess each round and develop goals and swing thoughts for the next round.

Following are some explanations to help you complete your diary:

Difficulty of Course/Conditions: Tees used means championship, men's, ladies, etc. The slope is a number assigned to each course to help compare the difficulty of one course to another; this is usually available on the course scorecard. Under course difficulty, indicate how this course compares to other courses you play (easy, average, hard). Were the hole locations particularly easy or hard?

Course conditions refer to the speed and smoothness of the greens and the condition of bunkers, fairways, and rough. Playing conditions may include time (like early morning) and weather (wind or dew, for example), but may also reflect whether winter rules were adopted, mulligans were used, or gimmes were taken. Nature of play may indicate if play was particularly slow or rushed or if playing partners got on your nerves.

Performance Ratings: Rate various aspects of your physical and mental game on a scale of your choice. For example, you might use a scale from 1 to 10 where 10 is excellent, 5 is average, and 1 is poor, or you might write ++ for very good, + for good, 0 for average, - for poor, and -- for very poor. Decide what works best for you. If you use 'other,' indicate what you are rating.

Goals: Record your goals, swing thoughts, and strategy for your round.

Key Shots: Describe memorable shots hit during the round. Close your eyes and visualize these good shots over and over – not just today, but review these in the future to draw from these positive moments.

Also describe shots that were unsatisfactory, but try not to visualize poor shots. Instead, imagine yourself in the same situations and visualize yourself hitting much better shots. You want to list areas needing improvement to help assess what you need to work on, but you want to visualize good shots, not poor shots.

Mental Toughness: This may include good or poor decisions made during the round. It can also include moments where you were over-confident, ideally confident, or lacked confidence in important situations. It may include moments where you broke down mentally, or used determination to rebound from a difficult situation. Lapses in concentration are also important to note. Again, learn from your mistakes, but focus on what you did right and showing better mental toughness next time.

Assessment: Assess whether or not you met your various goals and how your swing thoughts panned out. Identify areas that need improvement and work on these. Draw from the strengths you exhibited in this round to aid you in the future. Finally, adopt a set of goals and swing thoughts for the next round.

The End-of-Round Golf Diary

course: _Dogleg City, C.C._   date: _7/ 9 /08_ score: _84_

Difficulty of Course / Conditions

yardage: _6,532_ tees used: _white_ slope: _105_ course difficulty: _hard_

hole locations: _ave._ course conditions: _hard, fast, crusty_

playing conditions: _dry, windy, club rules_

nature of play: _very slow_   ailments: _back ache_

Performance Ratings

overall round performance: _4_   driving: _2_   fairway woods: _5_

long irons: _1_   mid-irons: _6_   short irons: _9_   wedges: _4_

pitching: _3_   sand play: _2_   chipping: _10_   lag putting: _4_

short putts: _8_   mid-range putts: _5_   other: _hybrids, 7_

patience: _6_   confidence: _8_   perseverance: _4_   focus: _5_

Goals

pre-round goals: _break 80, keep the same ball all day_

pre-round swing thoughts: _keep left arm straight, right elbow in_

pre-round short game thoughts: _keep head down through contact_

pre-round putting thoughts: _don't break wrists, read extra break_

pre-round strategy: _only use driver 5 times; lay up on #'s 6 and 13_

Key Shots

memorable shots: _hit 8-iron over the tree on #15 to within 7 ft._
sunk 30-footer on #9 from top of the green, broke 2 ft. left
reached #17 in two; a great birdie after losing it on #16
pitch over the bunker on #4; very crisp strike

Close your eyes and visualize good shots that you hit today. Repeat a few times.

shots needing improvement: _drove it short and right all day_
two bunker shots fat, one skulled
hit several pitches fat
not getting the long irons high enough

Visualize yourself in the same situations hitting good shots.

Mental Toughness

Describe good decisions made today, positive emotions, and other mental strengths:
good par on #6 after lay up; cooled down after losing temper on #16; good fairway wood off tee of #4 after poor start; good mood most of the day

Describe mental mistakes or lapses, but in your mind, focus on the good, not the bad:
drove it in the water on #16, lost cool and made triple bogey
hit driver on #13, wound up right behind the oak tree
got distracted on #5, hit birdie putt 8 ft. by

Assessment

Which goals did you meet? _almost kept the same ball; lost it on #16_
Which goals were not met? _didn't break 80, lost one ball_
How did your swing thoughts work? _worked well on full swings except for hitting low long irons; still broke wrists on some putts_
strengths from this round: _rebounded nicely after bad hole_
areas to work on: _driving, long irons, pitching, bunker play_
goals for next time: _stick to strategy; better swings with driver_
swing thoughts for next time: _fuller shoulder turn worked well at end_

course: _____ date: ___/___/___ score: _____

Difficulty of Course / Conditions

yardage: _____ tees used: _____ slope: _____ course difficulty: _____

hole locations: _____ course conditions: _____

playing conditions: _____

nature of play: _____ ailments: _____

Performance Ratings

overall round performance: _____ driving: _____ fairway woods: _____

long irons: _____ mid-irons: _____ short irons: _____ wedges: _____

pitching: _____ sand play: _____ chipping: _____ lag putting: _____

short putts: _____ mid-range putts: _____ other: _____

patience: _____ confidence: _____ perseverance: _____ focus: _____

Goals

pre-round goals: _____

pre-round swing thoughts: _____

pre-round short game thoughts: _____

pre-round putting thoughts: _____

pre-round strategy: _____

Key Shots

memorable shots: _____

_____

_____

_____

_____

_____

Close your eyes and visualize good shots that you hit today. Repeat a few times.

shots needing improvement: _____

_____

_____

_____

_____

_____

Visualize yourself in the same situations hitting good shots.

Mental Toughness

Describe good decisions made today, positive emotions, and other mental strengths:

_____

_____

_____

Describe mental mistakes or lapses, but in your mind, focus on the good, not the bad:

_____

_____

_____

Assessment

Which goals did you meet? _____

Which goals were not met? _____

How did your swing thoughts work? _____

_____

strengths from this round: _____

areas to work on: _____

goals for next time: _____

swing thoughts for next time: _____

course: _____ date: ___/___/___ score: _____

Difficulty of Course / Conditions

yardage: _____ tees used: _____ slope: _____ course difficulty: _____

hole locations: _____ course conditions: _____

playing conditions: _____

nature of play: _____ ailments: _____

Performance Ratings

overall round performance: _____ driving: _____ fairway woods: _____

long irons: _____ mid-irons: _____ short irons: _____ wedges: _____

pitching: _____ sand play: _____ chipping: _____ lag putting: _____

short putts: _____ mid-range putts: _____ other: _____

patience: _____ confidence: _____ perseverance: _____ focus: _____

Goals

pre-round goals: _____

pre-round swing thoughts: _____

pre-round short game thoughts: _____

pre-round putting thoughts: _____

pre-round strategy: _____

Key Shots

memorable shots: _____

_____

_____

_____

_____

_____

Close your eyes and visualize good shots that you hit today. Repeat a few times.

shots needing improvement: _____

_____

_____

_____

_____

_____

Visualize yourself in the same situations hitting good shots.

Mental Toughness

Describe good decisions made today, positive emotions, and other mental strengths:

_____

_____

_____

Describe mental mistakes or lapses, but in your mind, focus on the good, not the bad:

_____

_____

_____

Assessment

Which goals did you meet? _____

Which goals were not met? _____

How did your swing thoughts work? _____

_____

strengths from this round: _____

areas to work on: _____

goals for next time: _____

swing thoughts for next time: _____

course: _____ date: ___/___/___ score: _____

Difficulty of Course / Conditions

yardage: _____ tees used: _____ slope: _____ course difficulty: _____

hole locations: _____ course conditions: _____

playing conditions: _____

nature of play: _____ ailments: _____

Performance Ratings

overall round performance: _____ driving: _____ fairway woods: _____

long irons: _____ mid-irons: _____ short irons: _____ wedges: _____

pitching: _____ sand play: _____ chipping: _____ lag putting: _____

short putts: _____ mid-range putts: _____ other: _____

patience: _____ confidence: _____ perseverance: _____ focus: _____

Goals

pre-round goals: _____

pre-round swing thoughts: _____

pre-round short game thoughts: _____

pre-round putting thoughts: _____

pre-round strategy: _____

Key Shots

memorable shots: _____

_____

_____

_____

_____

_____

Close your eyes and visualize good shots that you hit today. Repeat a few times.

shots needing improvement: _____

_____

_____

_____

_____

_____

Visualize yourself in the same situations hitting good shots.

Mental Toughness

Describe good decisions made today, positive emotions, and other mental strengths:

_____

_____

_____

Describe mental mistakes or lapses, but in your mind, focus on the good, not the bad:

_____

_____

_____

Assessment

Which goals did you meet? _____

Which goals were not met? _____

How did your swing thoughts work? _____

_____

strengths from this round: _____

areas to work on: _____

goals for next time: _____

swing thoughts for next time: _____

course: _____ date: ___/___/___ score: _____

Difficulty of Course / Conditions

yardage: _____ tees used: _____ slope: _____ course difficulty: _____

hole locations: _____ course conditions: _____

playing conditions: _____

nature of play: _____ ailments: _____

Performance Ratings

overall round performance: _____ driving: _____ fairway woods: _____

long irons: _____ mid-irons: _____ short irons: _____ wedges: _____

pitching: _____ sand play: _____ chipping: _____ lag putting: _____

short putts: _____ mid-range putts: _____ other: _____

patience: _____ confidence: _____ perseverance: _____ focus: _____

Goals

pre-round goals: _____

pre-round swing thoughts: _____

pre-round short game thoughts: _____

pre-round putting thoughts: _____

pre-round strategy: _____

Key Shots

memorable shots: _____

_____

_____

_____

_____

_____

Close your eyes and visualize good shots that you hit today. Repeat a few times.

shots needing improvement: _____

_____

_____

_____

_____

_____

Visualize yourself in the same situations hitting good shots.

Mental Toughness

Describe good decisions made today, positive emotions, and other mental strengths:

_____

_____

_____

Describe mental mistakes or lapses, but in your mind, focus on the good, not the bad:

_____

_____

_____

Assessment

Which goals did you meet? _____

Which goals were not met? _____

How did your swing thoughts work? _____

_____

strengths from this round: _____

areas to work on: _____

goals for next time: _____

swing thoughts for next time: _____

course: _____ date: ___/___/___ score: _____

Difficulty of Course / Conditions

yardage: _____ tees used: _____ slope: _____ course difficulty: _____

hole locations: _____ course conditions: _____

playing conditions: _____

nature of play: _____ ailments: _____

Performance Ratings

overall round performance: _____ driving: _____ fairway woods: _____

long irons: _____ mid-irons: _____ short irons: _____ wedges: _____

pitching: _____ sand play: _____ chipping: _____ lag putting: _____

short putts: _____ mid-range putts: _____ other: _____

patience: _____ confidence: _____ perseverance: _____ focus: _____

Goals

pre-round goals: _____

pre-round swing thoughts: _____

pre-round short game thoughts: _____

pre-round putting thoughts: _____

pre-round strategy: _____

Key Shots

memorable shots: _____

_____

_____

_____

_____

_____

Close your eyes and visualize good shots that you hit today. Repeat a few times.

shots needing improvement: _____

_____

_____

_____

_____

_____

Visualize yourself in the same situations hitting good shots.

Mental Toughness

Describe good decisions made today, positive emotions, and other mental strengths:

_____

_____

_____

Describe mental mistakes or lapses, but in your mind, focus on the good, not the bad:

_____

_____

_____

Assessment

Which goals did you meet? _____

Which goals were not met? _____

How did your swing thoughts work? _____

_____

strengths from this round: _____

areas to work on: _____

goals for next time: _____

swing thoughts for next time: _____

course: _____ date: ___/___/___ score: _____

Difficulty of Course / Conditions

yardage: _____ tees used: _____ slope: _____ course difficulty: _____

hole locations: _____ course conditions: _____

playing conditions: _____

nature of play: _____ ailments: _____

Performance Ratings

overall round performance: _____ driving: _____ fairway woods: _____

long irons: _____ mid-irons: _____ short irons: _____ wedges: _____

pitching: _____ sand play: _____ chipping: _____ lag putting: _____

short putts: _____ mid-range putts: _____ other: _____

patience: _____ confidence: _____ perseverance: _____ focus: _____

Goals

pre-round goals: _____

pre-round swing thoughts: _____

pre-round short game thoughts: _____

pre-round putting thoughts: _____

pre-round strategy: _____

Key Shots

memorable shots: _____

_____

_____

_____

_____

_____

Close your eyes and visualize good shots that you hit today. Repeat a few times.

shots needing improvement: _____

_____

_____

_____

_____

_____

Visualize yourself in the same situations hitting good shots.

Mental Toughness

Describe good decisions made today, positive emotions, and other mental strengths:

_____

_____

_____

Describe mental mistakes or lapses, but in your mind, focus on the good, not the bad:

_____

_____

_____

Assessment

Which goals did you meet? _____

Which goals were not met? _____

How did your swing thoughts work? _____

_____

strengths from this round: _____

areas to work on: _____

goals for next time: _____

swing thoughts for next time: _____

course: _____ date: ___/___/___ score: _____

Difficulty of Course / Conditions

yardage: _____ tees used: _____ slope: _____ course difficulty: _____

hole locations: _____ course conditions: _____

playing conditions: _____

nature of play: _____ ailments: _____

Performance Ratings

overall round performance: _____ driving: _____ fairway woods: _____

long irons: _____ mid-irons: _____ short irons: _____ wedges: _____

pitching: _____ sand play: _____ chipping: _____ lag putting: _____

short putts: _____ mid-range putts: _____ other: _____

patience: _____ confidence: _____ perseverance: _____ focus: _____

Goals

pre-round goals: _____

pre-round swing thoughts: _____

pre-round short game thoughts: _____

pre-round putting thoughts: _____

pre-round strategy: _____

Key Shots

memorable shots: _____

_____

_____

_____

_____

_____

Close your eyes and visualize good shots that you hit today. Repeat a few times.

The End-of-Round Golf Diary

shots needing improvement: _____

_____
_____
_____
_____
_____

Visualize yourself in the same situations hitting good shots.

Mental Toughness

Describe good decisions made today, positive emotions, and other mental strengths:

_____
_____
_____

Describe mental mistakes or lapses, but in your mind, focus on the good, not the bad:

_____
_____
_____

Assessment

Which goals did you meet? _____

Which goals were not met? _____

How did your swing thoughts work? _____

_____

strengths from this round: _____

areas to work on: _____

goals for next time: _____

swing thoughts for next time: _____

course: _____ date: ___/___/___ score: _____

Difficulty of Course / Conditions

yardage: _____ tees used: _____ slope: _____ course difficulty: _____

hole locations: _____ course conditions: _____

playing conditions: _____

nature of play: _____ ailments: _____

Performance Ratings

overall round performance: _____ driving: _____ fairway woods: _____

long irons: _____ mid-irons: _____ short irons: _____ wedges: _____

pitching: _____ sand play: _____ chipping: _____ lag putting: _____

short putts: _____ mid-range putts: _____ other: _____

patience: _____ confidence: _____ perseverance: _____ focus: _____

Goals

pre-round goals: _____

pre-round swing thoughts: _____

pre-round short game thoughts: _____

pre-round putting thoughts: _____

pre-round strategy: _____

Key Shots

memorable shots: _____

_____

_____

_____

_____

_____

Close your eyes and visualize good shots that you hit today. Repeat a few times.

shots needing improvement: _____

_____

_____

_____

_____

_____

Visualize yourself in the same situations hitting good shots.

Mental Toughness

Describe good decisions made today, positive emotions, and other mental strengths:

_____

_____

_____

Describe mental mistakes or lapses, but in your mind, focus on the good, not the bad:

_____

_____

_____

Assessment

Which goals did you meet? _____

Which goals were not met? _____

How did your swing thoughts work? _____

_____

strengths from this round: _____

areas to work on: _____

goals for next time: _____

swing thoughts for next time: _____

course: _____ date: ___/___/___ score: _____

Difficulty of Course / Conditions

yardage: _____ tees used: _____ slope: _____ course difficulty: _____

hole locations: _____ course conditions: _____

playing conditions: _____

nature of play: _____ ailments: _____

Performance Ratings

overall round performance: _____ driving: _____ fairway woods: _____

long irons: _____ mid-irons: _____ short irons: _____ wedges: _____

pitching: _____ sand play: _____ chipping: _____ lag putting: _____

short putts: _____ mid-range putts: _____ other: _____

patience: _____ confidence: _____ perseverance: _____ focus: _____

Goals

pre-round goals: _____

pre-round swing thoughts: _____

pre-round short game thoughts: _____

pre-round putting thoughts: _____

pre-round strategy: _____

Key Shots

memorable shots: _____

_____

_____

_____

_____

_____

Close your eyes and visualize good shots that you hit today. Repeat a few times.

shots needing improvement: _____

_____

_____

_____

_____

_____

Visualize yourself in the same situations hitting good shots.

Mental Toughness

Describe good decisions made today, positive emotions, and other mental strengths:

_____

_____

_____

Describe mental mistakes or lapses, but in your mind, focus on the good, not the bad:

_____

_____

_____

Assessment

Which goals did you meet? _____

Which goals were not met? _____

How did your swing thoughts work? _____

_____

strengths from this round: _____

areas to work on: _____

goals for next time: _____

swing thoughts for next time: _____

course: _____ date: ___/___/___ score: _____

Difficulty of Course / Conditions

yardage: _____ tees used: _____ slope: _____ course difficulty: _____

hole locations: _____ course conditions: _____

playing conditions: _____

nature of play: _____ ailments: _____

Performance Ratings

overall round performance: _____ driving: _____ fairway woods: _____

long irons: _____ mid-irons: _____ short irons: _____ wedges: _____

pitching: _____ sand play: _____ chipping: _____ lag putting: _____

short putts: _____ mid-range putts: _____ other: _____

patience: _____ confidence: _____ perseverance: _____ focus: _____

Goals

pre-round goals: _____

pre-round swing thoughts: _____

pre-round short game thoughts: _____

pre-round putting thoughts: _____

pre-round strategy: _____

Key Shots

memorable shots: _____

_____

_____

_____

_____

_____

Close your eyes and visualize good shots that you hit today. Repeat a few times.

shots needing improvement: _____

_____
_____
_____
_____
_____

Visualize yourself in the same situations hitting good shots.

Mental Toughness

Describe good decisions made today, positive emotions, and other mental strengths:

_____
_____
_____

Describe mental mistakes or lapses, but in your mind, focus on the good, not the bad:

_____
_____
_____

Assessment

Which goals did you meet? _____
Which goals were not met? _____
How did your swing thoughts work? _____

_____

strengths from this round: _____

areas to work on: _____

goals for next time: _____

swing thoughts for next time: _____

course: _____ date: ___/___/___ score: _____

Difficulty of Course / Conditions

yardage: _____ tees used: _____ slope: _____ course difficulty: _____

hole locations: _____ course conditions: _____

playing conditions: _____

nature of play: _____ ailments: _____

Performance Ratings

overall round performance: _____ driving: _____ fairway woods: _____

long irons: _____ mid-irons: _____ short irons: _____ wedges: _____

pitching: _____ sand play: _____ chipping: _____ lag putting: _____

short putts: _____ mid-range putts: _____ other: _____

patience: _____ confidence: _____ perseverance: _____ focus: _____

Goals

pre-round goals: _____

pre-round swing thoughts: _____

pre-round short game thoughts: _____

pre-round putting thoughts: _____

pre-round strategy: _____

Key Shots

memorable shots: _____

_____

_____

_____

_____

_____

Close your eyes and visualize good shots that you hit today. Repeat a few times.

shots needing improvement: _____

_____

_____

_____

_____

_____

Visualize yourself in the same situations hitting good shots.

Mental Toughness

Describe good decisions made today, positive emotions, and other mental strengths:

_____

_____

_____

Describe mental mistakes or lapses, but in your mind, focus on the good, not the bad:

_____

_____

_____

Assessment

Which goals did you meet? _____

Which goals were not met? _____

How did your swing thoughts work? _____

_____

strengths from this round: _____

areas to work on: _____

goals for next time: _____

swing thoughts for next time: _____

course: _____ date: ___/___/___ score: _____

Difficulty of Course / Conditions

yardage: _____ tees used: _____ slope: _____ course difficulty: _____

hole locations: _____ course conditions: _____

playing conditions: _____

nature of play: _____ ailments: _____

Performance Ratings

overall round performance: _____ driving: _____ fairway woods: _____

long irons: _____ mid-irons: _____ short irons: _____ wedges: _____

pitching: _____ sand play: _____ chipping: _____ lag putting: _____

short putts: _____ mid-range putts: _____ other: _____

patience: _____ confidence: _____ perseverance: _____ focus: _____

Goals

pre-round goals: _____

pre-round swing thoughts: _____

pre-round short game thoughts: _____

pre-round putting thoughts: _____

pre-round strategy: _____

Key Shots

memorable shots: _____

_____

_____

_____

_____

_____

Close your eyes and visualize good shots that you hit today. Repeat a few times.

shots needing improvement: _____

_____

_____

_____

_____

_____

Visualize yourself in the same situations hitting good shots.

Mental Toughness

Describe good decisions made today, positive emotions, and other mental strengths:

_____

_____

_____

Describe mental mistakes or lapses, but in your mind, focus on the good, not the bad:

_____

_____

_____

Assessment

Which goals did you meet? _____

Which goals were not met? _____

How did your swing thoughts work? _____

_____

strengths from this round: _____

areas to work on: _____

goals for next time: _____

swing thoughts for next time: _____

course: _____ date: ___/___/___ score: _____

Difficulty of Course / Conditions

yardage: _____ tees used: _____ slope: _____ course difficulty: _____

hole locations: _____ course conditions: _____

playing conditions: _____

nature of play: _____ ailments: _____

Performance Ratings

overall round performance: _____ driving: _____ fairway woods: _____

long irons: _____ mid-irons: _____ short irons: _____ wedges: _____

pitching: _____ sand play: _____ chipping: _____ lag putting: _____

short putts: _____ mid-range putts: _____ other: _____

patience: _____ confidence: _____ perseverance: _____ focus: _____

Goals

pre-round goals: _____

pre-round swing thoughts: _____

pre-round short game thoughts: _____

pre-round putting thoughts: _____

pre-round strategy: _____

Key Shots

memorable shots: _____

_____

_____

_____

_____

_____

Close your eyes and visualize good shots that you hit today. Repeat a few times.

shots needing improvement: _____

_____

_____

_____

_____

_____

Visualize yourself in the same situations hitting good shots.

Mental Toughness

Describe good decisions made today, positive emotions, and other mental strengths:

_____

_____

_____

Describe mental mistakes or lapses, but in your mind, focus on the good, not the bad:

_____

_____

_____

Assessment

Which goals did you meet? _____

Which goals were not met? _____

How did your swing thoughts work? _____

_____

strengths from this round: _____

areas to work on: _____

goals for next time: _____

swing thoughts for next time: _____

course: _____ date: ___/___/___ score: _____

Difficulty of Course / Conditions

yardage: _____ tees used: _____ slope: _____ course difficulty: _____

hole locations: _____ course conditions: _____

playing conditions: _____

nature of play: _____ ailments: _____

Performance Ratings

overall round performance: _____ driving: _____ fairway woods: _____

long irons: _____ mid-irons: _____ short irons: _____ wedges: _____

pitching: _____ sand play: _____ chipping: _____ lag putting: _____

short putts: _____ mid-range putts: _____ other: _____

patience: _____ confidence: _____ perseverance: _____ focus: _____

Goals

pre-round goals: _____

pre-round swing thoughts: _____

pre-round short game thoughts: _____

pre-round putting thoughts: _____

pre-round strategy: _____

Key Shots

memorable shots: _____

_____

_____

_____

_____

_____

Close your eyes and visualize good shots that you hit today. Repeat a few times.

shots needing improvement: _____

_____

_____

_____

_____

_____

Visualize yourself in the same situations hitting good shots.

Mental Toughness

Describe good decisions made today, positive emotions, and other mental strengths:

_____

_____

_____

Describe mental mistakes or lapses, but in your mind, focus on the good, not the bad:

_____

_____

_____

Assessment

Which goals did you meet? _____

Which goals were not met? _____

How did your swing thoughts work? _____

_____

strengths from this round: _____

areas to work on: _____

goals for next time: _____

swing thoughts for next time: _____

course: _____ date: ___/___/___ score: _____

Difficulty of Course / Conditions

yardage: _____ tees used: _____ slope: _____ course difficulty: _____

hole locations: _____ course conditions: _____

playing conditions: _____

nature of play: _____ ailments: _____

Performance Ratings

overall round performance: _____ driving: _____ fairway woods: _____

long irons: _____ mid-irons: _____ short irons: _____ wedges: _____

pitching: _____ sand play: _____ chipping: _____ lag putting: _____

short putts: _____ mid-range putts: _____ other: _____

patience: _____ confidence: _____ perseverance: _____ focus: _____

Goals

pre-round goals: _____

pre-round swing thoughts: _____

pre-round short game thoughts: _____

pre-round putting thoughts: _____

pre-round strategy: _____

Key Shots

memorable shots: _____

_____

_____

_____

_____

_____

Close your eyes and visualize good shots that you hit today. Repeat a few times.

shots needing improvement: _____

_____

_____

_____

_____

_____

Visualize yourself in the same situations hitting good shots.

Mental Toughness

Describe good decisions made today, positive emotions, and other mental strengths:

_____

_____

_____

Describe mental mistakes or lapses, but in your mind, focus on the good, not the bad:

_____

_____

_____

Assessment

Which goals did you meet? _____

Which goals were not met? _____

How did your swing thoughts work? _____

_____

strengths from this round: _____

areas to work on: _____

goals for next time: _____

swing thoughts for next time: _____

course: _____ date: ___/___/___ score: _____

Difficulty of Course / Conditions

yardage: _____ tees used: _____ slope: _____ course difficulty: _____

hole locations: _____ course conditions: _____

playing conditions: _____

nature of play: _____ ailments: _____

Performance Ratings

overall round performance: _____ driving: _____ fairway woods: _____

long irons: _____ mid-irons: _____ short irons: _____ wedges: _____

pitching: _____ sand play: _____ chipping: _____ lag putting: _____

short putts: _____ mid-range putts: _____ other: _____

patience: _____ confidence: _____ perseverance: _____ focus: _____

Goals

pre-round goals: _____

pre-round swing thoughts: _____

pre-round short game thoughts: _____

pre-round putting thoughts: _____

pre-round strategy: _____

Key Shots

memorable shots: _____

_____

_____

_____

_____

_____

Close your eyes and visualize good shots that you hit today. Repeat a few times.

shots needing improvement: _____

_____

_____

_____

_____

_____

Visualize yourself in the same situations hitting good shots.

Mental Toughness

Describe good decisions made today, positive emotions, and other mental strengths:

_____

_____

_____

Describe mental mistakes or lapses, but in your mind, focus on the good, not the bad:

_____

_____

_____

Assessment

Which goals did you meet? _____

Which goals were not met? _____

How did your swing thoughts work? _____

_____

strengths from this round: _____

areas to work on: _____

goals for next time: _____

swing thoughts for next time: _____

course: _____ date: ___/___/___ score: _____

Difficulty of Course / Conditions

yardage: _____ tees used: _____ slope: _____ course difficulty: _____

hole locations: _____ course conditions: _____

playing conditions: _____

nature of play: _____ ailments: _____

Performance Ratings

overall round performance: _____ driving: _____ fairway woods: _____

long irons: _____ mid-irons: _____ short irons: _____ wedges: _____

pitching: _____ sand play: _____ chipping: _____ lag putting: _____

short putts: _____ mid-range putts: _____ other: _____

patience: _____ confidence: _____ perseverance: _____ focus: _____

Goals

pre-round goals: _____

pre round swing thoughts: _____

pre-round short game thoughts: _____

pre-round putting thoughts: _____

pre-round strategy: _____

Key Shots

memorable shots: _____

_____

_____

_____

_____

_____

Close your eyes and visualize good shots that you hit today. Repeat a few times.

shots needing improvement: _____

_____

_____

_____

_____

_____

Visualize yourself in the same situations hitting good shots.

Mental Toughness

Describe good decisions made today, positive emotions, and other mental strengths:

_____

_____

_____

Describe mental mistakes or lapses, but in your mind, focus on the good, not the bad:

_____

_____

_____

Assessment

Which goals did you meet? _____

Which goals were not met? _____

How did your swing thoughts work? _____

_____

strengths from this round: _____

areas to work on: _____

goals for next time: _____

swing thoughts for next time: _____

course: _____ date: ___/___/___ score: _____

Difficulty of Course / Conditions

yardage: _____ tees used: _____ slope: _____ course difficulty: _____

hole locations: _____ course conditions: _____

playing conditions: _____

nature of play: _____ ailments: _____

Performance Ratings

overall round performance: _____ driving: _____ fairway woods: _____

long irons: _____ mid-irons: _____ short irons: _____ wedges: _____

pitching: _____ sand play: _____ chipping: _____ lag putting: _____

short putts: _____ mid-range putts: _____ other: _____

patience: _____ confidence: _____ perseverance: _____ focus: _____

Goals

pre-round goals: _____

pre-round swing thoughts: _____

pre-round short game thoughts: _____

pre-round putting thoughts: _____

pre-round strategy: _____

Key Shots

memorable shots: _____

_____

_____

_____

_____

_____

Close your eyes and visualize good shots that you hit today. Repeat a few times.

shots needing improvement: _____

_____

_____

_____

_____

_____

_____

Visualize yourself in the same situations hitting good shots.

Mental Toughness

Describe good decisions made today, positive emotions, and other mental strengths:

_____

_____

_____

Describe mental mistakes or lapses, but in your mind, focus on the good, not the bad:

_____

_____

_____

Assessment

Which goals did you meet? _____

Which goals were not met? _____

How did your swing thoughts work? _____

_____

strengths from this round: _____

areas to work on: _____

goals for next time: _____

swing thoughts for next time: _____

course: _____ date: ___/___/___ score: _____

Difficulty of Course / Conditions

yardage: _____ tees used: _____ slope: _____ course difficulty: _____

hole locations: _____ course conditions: _____

playing conditions: _____

nature of play: _____ ailments: _____

Performance Ratings

overall round performance: _____ driving: _____ fairway woods: _____

long irons: _____ mid-irons: _____ short irons: _____ wedges: _____

pitching: _____ sand play: _____ chipping: _____ lag putting: _____

short putts: _____ mid-range putts: _____ other: _____

patience: _____ confidence: _____ perseverance: _____ focus: _____

Goals

pre-round goals: _____

pre-round swing thoughts: _____

pre-round short game thoughts: _____

pre-round putting thoughts: _____

pre-round strategy: _____

Key Shots

memorable shots: _____

_____

_____

_____

_____

Close your eyes and visualize good shots that you hit today. Repeat a few times.

shots needing improvement: _____

_____

_____

_____

_____

_____

Visualize yourself in the same situations hitting good shots.

Mental Toughness

Describe good decisions made today, positive emotions, and other mental strengths:

_____

_____

_____

Describe mental mistakes or lapses, but in your mind, focus on the good, not the bad:

_____

_____

_____

Assessment

Which goals did you meet? _____

Which goals were not met? _____

How did your swing thoughts work? _____

_____

strengths from this round: _____

areas to work on: _____

goals for next time: _____

swing thoughts for next time: _____

course: _____ date: ___/___/___ score: _____

Difficulty of Course / Conditions

yardage: _____ tees used: _____ slope: _____ course difficulty: _____

hole locations: _____ course conditions: _____

playing conditions: _____

nature of play: _____ ailments: _____

Performance Ratings

overall round performance: _____ driving: _____ fairway woods: _____

long irons: _____ mid-irons: _____ short irons: _____ wedges: _____

pitching: _____ sand play: _____ chipping: _____ lag putting: _____

short putts: _____ mid-range putts: _____ other: _____

patience: _____ confidence: _____ perseverance: _____ focus: _____

Goals

pre-round goals: _____

pre round swing thoughts: _____

pre-round short game thoughts: _____

pre-round putting thoughts: _____

pre-round strategy: _____

Key Shots

memorable shots: _____

_____

_____

_____

_____

_____

Close your eyes and visualize good shots that you hit today. Repeat a few times.

shots needing improvement: _____

_____

_____

_____

_____

_____

Visualize yourself in the same situations hitting good shots.

Mental Toughness

Describe good decisions made today, positive emotions, and other mental strengths:

_____

_____

_____

Describe mental mistakes or lapses, but in your mind, focus on the good, not the bad:

_____

_____

_____

Assessment

Which goals did you meet? _____

Which goals were not met? _____

How did your swing thoughts work? _____

_____

strengths from this round: _____

areas to work on: _____

goals for next time: _____

swing thoughts for next time: _____

course: _____ date: ___/___/___ score: _____

Difficulty of Course / Conditions

yardage: _____ tees used: _____ slope: _____ course difficulty: _____

hole locations: _____ course conditions: _____

playing conditions: _____

nature of play: _____ ailments: _____

Performance Ratings

overall round performance: _____ driving: _____ fairway woods: _____

long irons: _____ mid-irons: _____ short irons: _____ wedges: _____

pitching: _____ sand play: _____ chipping: _____ lag putting: _____

short putts: _____ mid-range putts: _____ other: _____

patience: _____ confidence: _____ perseverance: _____ focus: _____

Goals

pre-round goals: _____

pre-round swing thoughts: _____

pre-round short game thoughts: _____

pre-round putting thoughts: _____

pre-round strategy: _____

Key Shots

memorable shots: _____

_____

_____

_____

_____

_____

Close your eyes and visualize good shots that you hit today. Repeat a few times.

shots needing improvement: _____

_____
_____
_____
_____
_____

Visualize yourself in the same situations hitting good shots.

Mental Toughness

Describe good decisions made today, positive emotions, and other mental strengths:

_____
_____
_____

Describe mental mistakes or lapses, but in your mind, focus on the good, not the bad:

_____
_____
_____

Assessment

Which goals did you meet? _____
Which goals were not met? _____
How did your swing thoughts work? _____
_____

strengths from this round: _____

areas to work on: _____

goals for next time: _____

swing thoughts for next time: _____

course: _____ date: ___/___/___ score: _____

Difficulty of Course / Conditions

yardage: _____ tees used: _____ slope: _____ course difficulty: _____

hole locations: _____ course conditions: _____

playing conditions: _____

nature of play: _____ ailments: _____

Performance Ratings

overall round performance: _____ driving: _____ fairway woods: _____

long irons: _____ mid-irons: _____ short irons: _____ wedges: _____

pitching: _____ sand play: _____ chipping: _____ lag putting: _____

short putts: _____ mid-range putts: _____ other: _____

patience: _____ confidence: _____ perseverance: _____ focus: _____

Goals

pre-round goals: _____

pre-round swing thoughts: _____

pre-round short game thoughts: _____

pre-round putting thoughts: _____

pre-round strategy: _____

Key Shots

memorable shots: _____

_____

_____

_____

_____

_____

Close your eyes and visualize good shots that you hit today. Repeat a few times.

shots needing improvement: _____

_____

_____

_____

_____

_____

Visualize yourself in the same situations hitting good shots.

Mental Toughness

Describe good decisions made today, positive emotions, and other mental strengths:

_____

_____

_____

Describe mental mistakes or lapses, but in your mind, focus on the good, not the bad:

_____

_____

_____

Assessment

Which goals did you meet? _____

Which goals were not met? _____

How did your swing thoughts work? _____

_____

strengths from this round: _____

areas to work on: _____

goals for next time: _____

swing thoughts for next time: _____

course: _____ date: ___/___/___ score: _____

Difficulty of Course / Conditions

yardage: _____ tees used: _____ slope: _____ course difficulty: _____

hole locations: _____ course conditions: _____

playing conditions: _____

nature of play: _____ ailments: _____

Performance Ratings

overall round performance: _____ driving: _____ fairway woods: _____

long irons: _____ mid-irons: _____ short irons: _____ wedges: _____

pitching: _____ sand play: _____ chipping: _____ lag putting: _____

short putts: _____ mid-range putts: _____ other: _____

patience: _____ confidence: _____ perseverance: _____ focus: _____

Goals

pre-round goals: _____

pre-round swing thoughts: _____

pre-round short game thoughts: _____

pre-round putting thoughts: _____

pre-round strategy: _____

Key Shots

memorable shots: _____

_____

_____

_____

_____

Close your eyes and visualize good shots that you hit today. Repeat a few times.

shots needing improvement: _____

_____

_____

_____

_____

_____

Visualize yourself in the same situations hitting good shots.

Mental Toughness

Describe good decisions made today, positive emotions, and other mental strengths:

_____

_____

_____

Describe mental mistakes or lapses, but in your mind, focus on the good, not the bad:

_____

_____

_____

Assessment

Which goals did you meet? _____

Which goals were not met? _____

How did your swing thoughts work? _____

_____

strengths from this round: _____

areas to work on: _____

goals for next time: _____

swing thoughts for next time: _____

course: _____ date: __/__/__ score: _____

Difficulty of Course / Conditions

yardage: _____ tees used: _____ slope: _____ course difficulty: _____

hole locations: _____ course conditions: _____

playing conditions: _____

nature of play: _____ ailments: _____

Performance Ratings

overall round performance: _____ driving: _____ fairway woods: _____

long irons: _____ mid-irons: _____ short irons: _____ wedges: _____

pitching: _____ sand play: _____ chipping: _____ lag putting: _____

short putts: _____ mid-range putts: _____ other: _____

patience: _____ confidence: _____ perseverance: _____ focus: _____

Goals

pre-round goals: _____

pre round swing thoughts: _____

pre-round short game thoughts: _____

pre-round putting thoughts: _____

pre-round strategy: _____

Key Shots

memorable shots: _____

_____

_____

_____

_____

_____

Close your eyes and visualize good shots that you hit today. Repeat a few times.

shots needing improvement: _____

_____

_____

_____

_____

_____

Visualize yourself in the same situations hitting good shots.

Mental Toughness

Describe good decisions made today, positive emotions, and other mental strengths:

_____

_____

_____

Describe mental mistakes or lapses, but in your mind, focus on the good, not the bad:

_____

_____

_____

Assessment

Which goals did you meet? _____

Which goals were not met? _____

How did your swing thoughts work? _____

_____

strengths from this round: _____

areas to work on: _____

goals for next time: _____

swing thoughts for next time: _____

course: _____ date: ___/___/___ score: _____

Difficulty of Course / Conditions

yardage: _____ tees used: _____ slope: _____ course difficulty: _____

hole locations: _____ course conditions: _____

playing conditions: _____

nature of play: _____ ailments: _____

Performance Ratings

overall round performance: _____ driving: _____ fairway woods: _____

long irons: _____ mid-irons: _____ short irons: _____ wedges: _____

pitching: _____ sand play: _____ chipping: _____ lag putting: _____

short putts: _____ mid-range putts: _____ other: _____

patience: _____ confidence: _____ perseverance: _____ focus: _____

Goals

pre-round goals: _____

pre-round swing thoughts: _____

pre-round short game thoughts: _____

pre-round putting thoughts: _____

pre-round strategy: _____

Key Shots

memorable shots: _____

_____

_____

_____

_____

Close your eyes and visualize good shots that you hit today. Repeat a few times.

shots needing improvement: _____

_____

_____

_____

_____

_____

Visualize yourself in the same situations hitting good shots.

Mental Toughness

Describe good decisions made today, positive emotions, and other mental strengths:

_____

_____

_____

Describe mental mistakes or lapses, but in your mind, focus on the good, not the bad:

_____

_____

_____

Assessment

Which goals did you meet? _____

Which goals were not met? _____

How did your swing thoughts work? _____

_____

strengths from this round: _____

areas to work on: _____

goals for next time: _____

swing thoughts for next time: _____

course: _____ date: ___/___/___ score: _____

Difficulty of Course / Conditions

yardage: _____ tees used: _____ slope: _____ course difficulty: _____

hole locations: _____ course conditions: _____

playing conditions: _____

nature of play: _____ ailments: _____

Performance Ratings

overall round performance: _____ driving: _____ fairway woods: _____

long irons: _____ mid-irons: _____ short irons: _____ wedges: _____

pitching: _____ sand play: _____ chipping: _____ lag putting: _____

short putts: _____ mid-range putts: _____ other: _____

patience: _____ confidence: _____ perseverance: _____ focus: _____

Goals

pre-round goals: _____

pre-round swing thoughts: _____

pre-round short game thoughts: _____

pre-round putting thoughts: _____

pre-round strategy: _____

Key Shots

memorable shots: _____

_____

_____

_____

_____

_____

Close your eyes and visualize good shots that you hit today. Repeat a few times.

shots needing improvement: _____

_____

_____

_____

_____

_____

Visualize yourself in the same situations hitting good shots.

Mental Toughness

Describe good decisions made today, positive emotions, and other mental strengths:

_____

_____

_____

Describe mental mistakes or lapses, but in your mind, focus on the good, not the bad:

_____

_____

_____

Assessment

Which goals did you meet? _____

Which goals were not met? _____

How did your swing thoughts work? _____

_____

strengths from this round: _____

areas to work on: _____

goals for next time: _____

swing thoughts for next time: _____

course: _____ date: ___/___/___ score: _____

Difficulty of Course / Conditions

yardage: _____ tees used: _____ slope: _____ course difficulty: _____

hole locations: _____ course conditions: _____

playing conditions: _____

nature of play: _____ ailments: _____

Performance Ratings

overall round performance: _____ driving: _____ fairway woods: _____

long irons: _____ mid-irons: _____ short irons: _____ wedges: _____

pitching: _____ sand play: _____ chipping: _____ lag putting: _____

short putts: _____ mid-range putts: _____ other: _____

patience: _____ confidence: _____ perseverance: _____ focus: _____

Goals

pre-round goals: _____

pre-round swing thoughts: _____

pre-round short game thoughts: _____

pre-round putting thoughts: _____

pre-round strategy: _____

Key Shots

memorable shots: _____

_____

_____

_____

_____

_____

Close your eyes and visualize good shots that you hit today. Repeat a few times.

shots needing improvement: _____

_____
_____
_____
_____
_____

Visualize yourself in the same situations hitting good shots.

Mental Toughness

Describe good decisions made today, positive emotions, and other mental strengths:

_____
_____
_____

Describe mental mistakes or lapses, but in your mind, focus on the good, not the bad:

_____
_____
_____

Assessment

Which goals did you meet? _____
Which goals were not met? _____
How did your swing thoughts work? _____
_____

strengths from this round: _____

areas to work on: _____

goals for next time: _____

swing thoughts for next time: _____

course: _____ date: ___/___/___ score: _____

Difficulty of Course / Conditions

yardage: _____ tees used: _____ slope: _____ course difficulty: _____

hole locations: _____ course conditions: _____

playing conditions: _____

nature of play: _____ ailments: _____

Performance Ratings

overall round performance: _____ driving: _____ fairway woods: _____

long irons: _____ mid-irons: _____ short irons: _____ wedges: _____

pitching: _____ sand play: _____ chipping: _____ lag putting: _____

short putts: _____ mid-range putts: _____ other: _____

patience: _____ confidence: _____ perseverance: _____ focus: _____

Goals

pre-round goals: _____

pre-round swing thoughts: _____

pre-round short game thoughts: _____

pre-round putting thoughts: _____

pre-round strategy: _____

Key Shots

memorable shots: _____

_____

_____

_____

_____

_____

Close your eyes and visualize good shots that you hit today. Repeat a few times.

shots needing improvement: _____

_____

_____

_____

_____

_____

Visualize yourself in the same situations hitting good shots.

Mental Toughness

Describe good decisions made today, positive emotions, and other mental strengths:

_____

_____

_____

Describe mental mistakes or lapses, but in your mind, focus on the good, not the bad:

_____

_____

_____

Assessment

Which goals did you meet? _____

Which goals were not met? _____

How did your swing thoughts work? _____

_____

strengths from this round: _____

areas to work on: _____

goals for next time: _____

swing thoughts for next time: _____

course: _____ date: ___/___/___ score: _____

Difficulty of Course / Conditions

yardage: _____ tees used: _____ slope: _____ course difficulty: _____

hole locations: _____ course conditions: _____

playing conditions: _____

nature of play: _____ ailments: _____

Performance Ratings

overall round performance: _____ driving: _____ fairway woods: _____

long irons: _____ mid-irons: _____ short irons: _____ wedges: _____

pitching: _____ sand play: _____ chipping: _____ lag putting: _____

short putts: _____ mid-range putts: _____ other: _____

patience: _____ confidence: _____ perseverance: _____ focus: _____

Goals

pre-round goals: _____

pre-round swing thoughts: _____

pre-round short game thoughts: _____

pre-round putting thoughts: _____

pre-round strategy: _____

Key Shots

memorable shots: _____

_____

_____

_____

_____

_____

Close your eyes and visualize good shots that you hit today. Repeat a few times.

shots needing improvement: _____

_____
_____
_____
_____
_____

Visualize yourself in the same situations hitting good shots.

Mental Toughness

Describe good decisions made today, positive emotions, and other mental strengths:

_____
_____
_____

Describe mental mistakes or lapses, but in your mind, focus on the good, not the bad:

_____
_____
_____

Assessment

Which goals did you meet? _____
Which goals were not met? _____
How did your swing thoughts work? _____
_____

strengths from this round: _____

areas to work on: _____

goals for next time: _____

swing thoughts for next time: _____

course: _____ date: ___/___/___ score: _____

Difficulty of Course / Conditions

yardage: _____ tees used: _____ slope: _____ course difficulty: _____

hole locations: _____ course conditions: _____

playing conditions: _____

nature of play: _____ ailments: _____

Performance Ratings

overall round performance: _____ driving: _____ fairway woods: _____

long irons: _____ mid-irons: _____ short irons: _____ wedges: _____

pitching: _____ sand play: _____ chipping: _____ lag putting: _____

short putts: _____ mid-range putts: _____ other: _____

patience: _____ confidence: _____ perseverance: _____ focus: _____

Goals

pre-round goals: _____

pre-round swing thoughts: _____

pre-round short game thoughts: _____

pre-round putting thoughts: _____

pre-round strategy: _____

Key Shots

memorable shots: _____

_____

_____

_____

_____

_____

Close your eyes and visualize good shots that you hit today. Repeat a few times.

shots needing improvement: _____

_____

_____

_____

_____

_____

Visualize yourself in the same situations hitting good shots.

Mental Toughness

Describe good decisions made today, positive emotions, and other mental strengths:

_____

_____

_____

Describe mental mistakes or lapses, but in your mind, focus on the good, not the bad:

_____

_____

_____

Assessment

Which goals did you meet? _____

Which goals were not met? _____

How did your swing thoughts work? _____

_____

strengths from this round: _____

areas to work on: _____

goals for next time: _____

swing thoughts for next time: _____

course: _____ date: ___/___/___ score: _____

Difficulty of Course / Conditions

yardage: _____ tees used: _____ slope: _____ course difficulty: _____

hole locations: _____ course conditions: _____

playing conditions: _____

nature of play: _____ ailments: _____

Performance Ratings

overall round performance: _____ driving: _____ fairway woods: _____

long irons: _____ mid-irons: _____ short irons: _____ wedges: _____

pitching: _____ sand play: _____ chipping: _____ lag putting: _____

short putts: _____ mid-range putts: _____ other: _____

patience: _____ confidence: _____ perseverance: _____ focus: _____

Goals

pre-round goals: _____

pre-round swing thoughts: _____

pre-round short game thoughts: _____

pre-round putting thoughts: _____

pre-round strategy: _____

Key Shots

memorable shots: _____

_____

_____

_____

_____

_____

Close your eyes and visualize good shots that you hit today. Repeat a few times.

shots needing improvement: _____

_____

_____

_____

_____

_____

Visualize yourself in the same situations hitting good shots.

Mental Toughness

Describe good decisions made today, positive emotions, and other mental strengths:

_____

_____

_____

Describe mental mistakes or lapses, but in your mind, focus on the good, not the bad:

_____

_____

_____

Assessment

Which goals did you meet? _____

Which goals were not met? _____

How did your swing thoughts work? _____

_____

strengths from this round: _____

areas to work on: _____

goals for next time: _____

swing thoughts for next time: _____

course: _____ date: ___/___/___ score: _____

Difficulty of Course / Conditions

yardage: _____ tees used: _____ slope: _____ course difficulty: _____

hole locations: _____ course conditions: _____

playing conditions: _____

nature of play: _____ ailments: _____

Performance Ratings

overall round performance: _____ driving: _____ fairway woods: _____

long irons: _____ mid-irons: _____ short irons: _____ wedges: _____

pitching: _____ sand play: _____ chipping: _____ lag putting: _____

short putts: _____ mid-range putts: _____ other: _____

patience: _____ confidence: _____ perseverance: _____ focus: _____

Goals

pre-round goals: _____

pre-round swing thoughts: _____

pre-round short game thoughts: _____

pre-round putting thoughts: _____

pre-round strategy: _____

Key Shots

memorable shots: _____

_____

_____

_____

_____

_____

Close your eyes and visualize good shots that you hit today. Repeat a few times.

shots needing improvement: _____

_____

_____

_____

_____

_____

Visualize yourself in the same situations hitting good shots.

Mental Toughness

Describe good decisions made today, positive emotions, and other mental strengths:

_____

_____

_____

Describe mental mistakes or lapses, but in your mind, focus on the good, not the bad:

_____

_____

_____

Assessment

Which goals did you meet? _____

Which goals were not met? _____

How did your swing thoughts work? _____

_____

strengths from this round: _____

areas to work on: _____

goals for next time: _____

swing thoughts for next time: _____

course: _____ date: ___/___/___ score: _____

Difficulty of Course / Conditions

yardage: _____ tees used: _____ slope: _____ course difficulty: _____

hole locations: _____ course conditions: _____

playing conditions: _____

nature of play: _____ ailments: _____

Performance Ratings

overall round performance: _____ driving: _____ fairway woods: _____

long irons: _____ mid-irons: _____ short irons: _____ wedges: _____

pitching: _____ sand play: _____ chipping: _____ lag putting: _____

short putts: _____ mid-range putts: _____ other: _____

patience: _____ confidence: _____ perseverance: _____ focus: _____

Goals

pre-round goals: _____

pre-round swing thoughts: _____

pre-round short game thoughts: _____

pre-round putting thoughts: _____

pre-round strategy: _____

Key Shots

memorable shots: _____

_____

_____

_____

_____

_____

Close your eyes and visualize good shots that you hit today. Repeat a few times.

shots needing improvement: _____

_____

_____

_____

_____

_____

Visualize yourself in the same situations hitting good shots.

Mental Toughness

Describe good decisions made today, positive emotions, and other mental strengths:

_____

_____

_____

Describe mental mistakes or lapses, but in your mind, focus on the good, not the bad:

_____

_____

_____

Assessment

Which goals did you meet? _____

Which goals were not met? _____

How did your swing thoughts work? _____

_____

strengths from this round: _____

areas to work on: _____

goals for next time: _____

swing thoughts for next time: _____

course: _____ date: ___/___/___ score: _____

Difficulty of Course / Conditions

yardage: _____ tees used: _____ slope: _____ course difficulty: _____

hole locations: _____ course conditions: _____

playing conditions: _____

nature of play: _____ ailments: _____

Performance Ratings

overall round performance: _____ driving: _____ fairway woods: _____

long irons: _____ mid-irons: _____ short irons: _____ wedges: _____

pitching: _____ sand play: _____ chipping: _____ lag putting: _____

short putts: _____ mid-range putts: _____ other: _____

patience: _____ confidence: _____ perseverance: _____ focus: _____

Goals

pre-round goals: _____

pre-round swing thoughts: _____

pre-round short game thoughts: _____

pre-round putting thoughts: _____

pre-round strategy: _____

Key Shots

memorable shots: _____

_____

_____

_____

_____

_____

Close your eyes and visualize good shots that you hit today. Repeat a few times.

shots needing improvement: _____

_____

_____

_____

_____

_____

Visualize yourself in the same situations hitting good shots.

Mental Toughness

Describe good decisions made today, positive emotions, and other mental strengths:

_____

_____

_____

Describe mental mistakes or lapses, but in your mind, focus on the good, not the bad:

_____

_____

_____

Assessment

Which goals did you meet? _____

Which goals were not met? _____

How did your swing thoughts work? _____

_____

strengths from this round: _____

areas to work on: _____

goals for next time: _____

swing thoughts for next time: _____

course: _____ date: ___/___/___ score: _____

Difficulty of Course / Conditions

yardage: _____ tees used: _____ slope: _____ course difficulty: _____

hole locations: _____ course conditions: _____

playing conditions: _____

nature of play: _____ ailments: _____

Performance Ratings

overall round performance: _____ driving: _____ fairway woods: _____

long irons: _____ mid-irons: _____ short irons: _____ wedges: _____

pitching: _____ sand play: _____ chipping: _____ lag putting: _____

short putts: _____ mid-range putts: _____ other: _____

patience: _____ confidence: _____ perseverance: _____ focus: _____

Goals

pre-round goals: _____

pre-round swing thoughts: _____

pre-round short game thoughts: _____

pre-round putting thoughts: _____

pre-round strategy: _____

Key Shots

memorable shots: _____

_____

_____

_____

_____

_____

Close your eyes and visualize good shots that you hit today. Repeat a few times.

shots needing improvement: _____

_____
_____
_____
_____
_____

Visualize yourself in the same situations hitting good shots.

Mental Toughness

Describe good decisions made today, positive emotions, and other mental strengths:

_____
_____
_____

Describe mental mistakes or lapses, but in your mind, focus on the good, not the bad:

_____
_____
_____

Assessment

Which goals did you meet? _____
Which goals were not met? _____
How did your swing thoughts work? _____
_____

strengths from this round: _____
areas to work on: _____
goals for next time: _____
swing thoughts for next time: _____

course: _____ date: ___/___/___ score: _____

Difficulty of Course / Conditions

yardage: _____ tees used: _____ slope: _____ course difficulty: _____

hole locations: _____ course conditions: _____

playing conditions: _____

nature of play: _____ ailments: _____

Performance Ratings

overall round performance: _____ driving: _____ fairway woods: _____

long irons: _____ mid-irons: _____ short irons: _____ wedges: _____

pitching: _____ sand play: _____ chipping: _____ lag putting: _____

short putts: _____ mid-range putts: _____ other: _____

patience: _____ confidence: _____ perseverance: _____ focus: _____

Goals

pre-round goals: _____

pre-round swing thoughts: _____

pre-round short game thoughts: _____

pre-round putting thoughts: _____

pre-round strategy: _____

Key Shots

memorable shots: _____

_____

_____

_____

_____

_____

Close your eyes and visualize good shots that you hit today. Repeat a few times.

shots needing improvement: _____

_____

_____

_____

_____

_____

Visualize yourself in the same situations hitting good shots.

Mental Toughness

Describe good decisions made today, positive emotions, and other mental strengths:

_____

_____

_____

Describe mental mistakes or lapses, but in your mind, focus on the good, not the bad:

_____

_____

_____

Assessment

Which goals did you meet? _____

Which goals were not met? _____

How did your swing thoughts work? _____

_____

strengths from this round: _____

areas to work on: _____

goals for next time: _____

swing thoughts for next time: _____

course: _____ date: ___/___/___ score: _____

Difficulty of Course / Conditions

yardage: _____ tees used: _____ slope: _____ course difficulty: _____

hole locations: _____ course conditions: _____

playing conditions: _____

nature of play: _____ ailments: _____

Performance Ratings

overall round performance: _____ driving: _____ fairway woods: _____

long irons: _____ mid-irons: _____ short irons: _____ wedges: _____

pitching: _____ sand play: _____ chipping: _____ lag putting: _____

short putts: _____ mid-range putts: _____ other: _____

patience: _____ confidence: _____ perseverance: _____ focus: _____

Goals

pre-round goals: _____

pre-round swing thoughts: _____

pre-round short game thoughts: _____

pre-round putting thoughts: _____

pre-round strategy: _____

Key Shots

memorable shots: _____

_____

_____

_____

_____

_____

Close your eyes and visualize good shots that you hit today. Repeat a few times.

shots needing improvement: _____

_____

_____

_____

_____

_____

Visualize yourself in the same situations hitting good shots.

Mental Toughness

Describe good decisions made today, positive emotions, and other mental strengths:

_____

_____

_____

Describe mental mistakes or lapses, but in your mind, focus on the good, not the bad:

_____

_____

_____

Assessment

Which goals did you meet? _____

Which goals were not met? _____

How did your swing thoughts work? _____

_____

strengths from this round: _____

areas to work on: _____

goals for next time: _____

swing thoughts for next time: _____

course: _____ date: ___/___/___ score: _____

Difficulty of Course / Conditions

yardage: _____ tees used: _____ slope: _____ course difficulty: _____

hole locations: _____ course conditions: _____

playing conditions: _____

nature of play: _____ ailments: _____

Performance Ratings

overall round performance: _____ driving: _____ fairway woods: _____

long irons: _____ mid-irons: _____ short irons: _____ wedges: _____

pitching: _____ sand play: _____ chipping: _____ lag putting: _____

short putts: _____ mid-range putts: _____ other: _____

patience: _____ confidence: _____ perseverance: _____ focus: _____

Goals

pre-round goals: _____

pre-round swing thoughts: _____

pre-round short game thoughts: _____

pre-round putting thoughts: _____

pre-round strategy: _____

Key Shots

memorable shots: _____

_____

_____

_____

_____

_____

Close your eyes and visualize good shots that you hit today. Repeat a few times.

shots needing improvement: _____

_____
_____
_____
_____
_____
_____

Visualize yourself in the same situations hitting good shots.

Mental Toughness

Describe good decisions made today, positive emotions, and other mental strengths:

_____
_____
_____

Describe mental mistakes or lapses, but in your mind, focus on the good, not the bad:

_____
_____
_____

Assessment

Which goals did you meet? _____
Which goals were not met? _____
How did your swing thoughts work? _____
_____

strengths from this round: _____
areas to work on: _____
goals for next time: _____
swing thoughts for next time: _____

course: _____ date: ___/___/___ score: _____

Difficulty of Course / Conditions

yardage: _____ tees used: _____ slope: _____ course difficulty: _____

hole locations: _____ course conditions: _____

playing conditions: _____

nature of play: _____ ailments: _____

Performance Ratings

overall round performance: _____ driving: _____ fairway woods: _____

long irons: _____ mid-irons: _____ short irons: _____ wedges: _____

pitching: _____ sand play: _____ chipping: _____ lag putting: _____

short putts: _____ mid-range putts: _____ other: _____

patience: _____ confidence: _____ perseverance: _____ focus: _____

Goals

pre-round goals: _____

pre-round swing thoughts: _____

pre-round short game thoughts: _____

pre-round putting thoughts: _____

pre-round strategy: _____

Key Shots

memorable shots: _____

_____

_____

_____

_____

_____

Close your eyes and visualize good shots that you hit today. Repeat a few times.

shots needing improvement: _____

_____

_____

_____

_____

_____

Visualize yourself in the same situations hitting good shots.

Mental Toughness

Describe good decisions made today, positive emotions, and other mental strengths:

_____

_____

_____

Describe mental mistakes or lapses, but in your mind, focus on the good, not the bad:

_____

_____

_____

Assessment

Which goals did you meet? _____

Which goals were not met? _____

How did your swing thoughts work? _____

_____

strengths from this round: _____

areas to work on: _____

goals for next time: _____

swing thoughts for next time: _____

course: _____ date: ___/___/___ score: _____

Difficulty of Course / Conditions

yardage: _____ tees used: _____ slope: _____ course difficulty: _____

hole locations: _____ course conditions: _____

playing conditions: _____

nature of play: _____ ailments: _____

Performance Ratings

overall round performance: _____ driving: _____ fairway woods: _____

long irons: _____ mid-irons: _____ short irons: _____ wedges: _____

pitching: _____ sand play: _____ chipping: _____ lag putting: _____

short putts: _____ mid-range putts: _____ other: _____

patience: _____ confidence: _____ perseverance: _____ focus: _____

Goals

pre-round goals: _____

pre-round swing thoughts: _____

pre-round short game thoughts: _____

pre-round putting thoughts: _____

pre-round strategy: _____

Key Shots

memorable shots: _____

_____

_____

_____

_____

_____

Close your eyes and visualize good shots that you hit today. Repeat a few times.

shots needing improvement: _____

_____

_____

_____

_____

_____

_____

Visualize yourself in the same situations hitting good shots.

Mental Toughness

Describe good decisions made today, positive emotions, and other mental strengths:

_____

_____

_____

Describe mental mistakes or lapses, but in your mind, focus on the good, not the bad:

_____

_____

_____

Assessment

Which goals did you meet? _____

Which goals were not met? _____

How did your swing thoughts work? _____

_____

strengths from this round: _____

areas to work on: _____

goals for next time: _____

swing thoughts for next time: _____

course: _____ date: ___/___/___ score: _____

Difficulty of Course / Conditions

yardage: _____ tees used: _____ slope: _____ course difficulty: _____

hole locations: _____ course conditions: _____

playing conditions: _____

nature of play: _____ ailments: _____

Performance Ratings

overall round performance: _____ driving: _____ fairway woods: _____

long irons: _____ mid-irons: _____ short irons: _____ wedges: _____

pitching: _____ sand play: _____ chipping: _____ lag putting: _____

short putts: _____ mid-range putts: _____ other: _____

patience: _____ confidence: _____ perseverance: _____ focus: _____

Goals

pre-round goals: _____

pre-round swing thoughts: _____

pre-round short game thoughts: _____

pre-round putting thoughts: _____

pre-round strategy: _____

Key Shots

memorable shots: _____

_____

_____

_____

_____

_____

Close your eyes and visualize good shots that you hit today. Repeat a few times.

shots needing improvement: _____

_____

_____

_____

_____

_____

Visualize yourself in the same situations hitting good shots.

Mental Toughness

Describe good decisions made today, positive emotions, and other mental strengths:

_____

_____

_____

Describe mental mistakes or lapses, but in your mind, focus on the good, not the bad:

_____

_____

_____

Assessment

Which goals did you meet? _____

Which goals were not met? _____

How did your swing thoughts work? _____

_____

strengths from this round: _____

areas to work on: _____

goals for next time: _____

swing thoughts for next time: _____

course: _____ date: ___/___/___ score: _____

Difficulty of Course / Conditions

yardage: _____ tees used: _____ slope: _____ course difficulty: _____

hole locations: _____ course conditions: _____

playing conditions: _____

nature of play: _____ ailments: _____

Performance Ratings

overall round performance: _____ driving: _____ fairway woods: _____

long irons: _____ mid-irons: _____ short irons: _____ wedges: _____

pitching: _____ sand play: _____ chipping: _____ lag putting: _____

short putts: _____ mid-range putts: _____ other: _____

patience: _____ confidence: _____ perseverance: _____ focus: _____

Goals

pre-round goals: _____

pre-round swing thoughts: _____

pre-round short game thoughts: _____

pre-round putting thoughts: _____

pre-round strategy: _____

Key Shots

memorable shots: _____

_____

_____

_____

_____

_____

Close your eyes and visualize good shots that you hit today. Repeat a few times.

shots needing improvement: _____

_____

_____

_____

_____

_____

Visualize yourself in the same situations hitting good shots.

Mental Toughness

Describe good decisions made today, positive emotions, and other mental strengths:

_____

_____

_____

Describe mental mistakes or lapses, but in your mind, focus on the good, not the bad:

_____

_____

_____

Assessment

Which goals did you meet? _____
Which goals were not met? _____
How did your swing thoughts work? _____

_____

strengths from this round: _____

areas to work on: _____

goals for next time: _____

swing thoughts for next time: _____

course: _____ date: ___/___/___ score: _____

Difficulty of Course / Conditions

yardage: _____ tees used: _____ slope: _____ course difficulty: _____

hole locations: _____ course conditions: _____

playing conditions: _____

nature of play: _____ ailments: _____

Performance Ratings

overall round performance: _____ driving: _____ fairway woods: _____

long irons: _____ mid-irons: _____ short irons: _____ wedges: _____

pitching: _____ sand play: _____ chipping: _____ lag putting: _____

short putts: _____ mid-range putts: _____ other: _____

patience: _____ confidence: _____ perseverance: _____ focus: _____

Goals

pre-round goals: _____

pre-round swing thoughts: _____

pre-round short game thoughts: _____

pre-round putting thoughts: _____

pre-round strategy: _____

Key Shots

memorable shots: _____

_____

_____

_____

_____

_____

Close your eyes and visualize good shots that you hit today. Repeat a few times.

shots needing improvement: _____

_____

_____

_____

_____

_____

Visualize yourself in the same situations hitting good shots.

Mental Toughness

Describe good decisions made today, positive emotions, and other mental strengths:

_____

_____

_____

Describe mental mistakes or lapses, but in your mind, focus on the good, not the bad:

_____

_____

_____

Assessment

Which goals did you meet? _____

Which goals were not met? _____

How did your swing thoughts work? _____

_____

strengths from this round: _____

areas to work on: _____

goals for next time: _____

swing thoughts for next time: _____

course: _____ date: ___/___/___ score: _____

Difficulty of Course / Conditions

yardage: _____ tees used: _____ slope: _____ course difficulty: _____

hole locations: _____ course conditions: _____

playing conditions: _____

nature of play: _____ ailments: _____

Performance Ratings

overall round performance: _____ driving: _____ fairway woods: _____

long irons: _____ mid-irons: _____ short irons: _____ wedges: _____

pitching: _____ sand play: _____ chipping: _____ lag putting: _____

short putts: _____ mid-range putts: _____ other: _____

patience: _____ confidence: _____ perseverance: _____ focus: _____

Goals

pre-round goals: _____

pre-round swing thoughts: _____

pre-round short game thoughts: _____

pre-round putting thoughts: _____

pre-round strategy: _____

Key Shots

memorable shots: _____

_____

_____

_____

_____

_____

Close your eyes and visualize good shots that you hit today. Repeat a few times.

shots needing improvement: _____

_____

_____

_____

_____

_____

Visualize yourself in the same situations hitting good shots.

Mental Toughness

Describe good decisions made today, positive emotions, and other mental strengths:

_____

_____

_____

Describe mental mistakes or lapses, but in your mind, focus on the good, not the bad:

_____

_____

_____

Assessment

Which goals did you meet? _____

Which goals were not met? _____

How did your swing thoughts work? _____

_____

strengths from this round: _____

areas to work on: _____

goals for next time: _____

swing thoughts for next time: _____

course: _____ date: ___/___/___ score: _____

Difficulty of Course / Conditions

yardage: _____ tees used: _____ slope: _____ course difficulty: _____

hole locations: _____ course conditions: _____

playing conditions: _____

nature of play: _____ ailments: _____

Performance Ratings

overall round performance: _____ driving: _____ fairway woods: _____

long irons: _____ mid-irons: _____ short irons: _____ wedges: _____

pitching: _____ sand play: _____ chipping: _____ lag putting: _____

short putts: _____ mid-range putts: _____ other: _____

patience: _____ confidence: _____ perseverance: _____ focus: _____

Goals

pre-round goals: _____

pre-round swing thoughts: _____

pre-round short game thoughts: _____

pre-round putting thoughts: _____

pre-round strategy: _____

Key Shots

memorable shots: _____

_____

_____

_____

_____

_____

Close your eyes and visualize good shots that you hit today. Repeat a few times.

shots needing improvement: _____

_____

_____

_____

_____

_____

Visualize yourself in the same situations hitting good shots.

Mental Toughness

Describe good decisions made today, positive emotions, and other mental strengths:

_____

_____

_____

Describe mental mistakes or lapses, but in your mind, focus on the good, not the bad:

_____

_____

_____

Assessment

Which goals did you meet? _____

Which goals were not met? _____

How did your swing thoughts work? _____

_____

strengths from this round: _____

areas to work on: _____

goals for next time: _____

swing thoughts for next time: _____

course: _____ date: ___/___/___ score: _____

Difficulty of Course / Conditions

yardage: _____ tees used: _____ slope: _____ course difficulty: _____

hole locations: _____ course conditions: _____

playing conditions: _____

nature of play: _____ ailments: _____

Performance Ratings

overall round performance: _____ driving: _____ fairway woods: _____

long irons: _____ mid-irons: _____ short irons: _____ wedges: _____

pitching: _____ sand play: _____ chipping: _____ lag putting: _____

short putts: _____ mid-range putts: _____ other: _____

patience: _____ confidence: _____ perseverance: _____ focus: _____

Goals

pre-round goals: _____

pre-round swing thoughts: _____

pre-round short game thoughts: _____

pre-round putting thoughts: _____

pre-round strategy: _____

Key Shots

memorable shots: _____

_____

_____

_____

_____

Close your eyes and visualize good shots that you hit today. Repeat a few times.

shots needing improvement: _____

_____

_____

_____

_____

_____

Visualize yourself in the same situations hitting good shots.

Mental Toughness

Describe good decisions made today, positive emotions, and other mental strengths:

_____

_____

_____

Describe mental mistakes or lapses, but in your mind, focus on the good, not the bad:

_____

_____

_____

Assessment

Which goals did you meet? _____

Which goals were not met? _____

How did your swing thoughts work? _____

_____

strengths from this round: _____

areas to work on: _____

goals for next time: _____

swing thoughts for next time: _____

course: _____ date: ___/___/___ score: _____

Difficulty of Course / Conditions

yardage: _____ tees used: _____ slope: _____ course difficulty: _____

hole locations: _____ course conditions: _____

playing conditions: _____

nature of play: _____ ailments: _____

Performance Ratings

overall round performance: _____ driving: _____ fairway woods: _____

long irons: _____ mid-irons: _____ short irons: _____ wedges: _____

pitching: _____ sand play: _____ chipping: _____ lag putting: _____

short putts: _____ mid-range putts: _____ other: _____

patience: _____ confidence: _____ perseverance: _____ focus: _____

Goals

pre-round goals: _____

pre-round swing thoughts: _____

pre-round short game thoughts: _____

pre-round putting thoughts: _____

pre-round strategy: _____

Key Shots

memorable shots: _____

_____

_____

_____

_____

_____

Close your eyes and visualize good shots that you hit today. Repeat a few times.

shots needing improvement: _____

_____

_____

_____

_____

_____

_____

Visualize yourself in the same situations hitting good shots.

Mental Toughness

Describe good decisions made today, positive emotions, and other mental strengths:

_____

_____

_____

Describe mental mistakes or lapses, but in your mind, focus on the good, not the bad:

_____

_____

_____

Assessment

Which goals did you meet? _____

Which goals were not met? _____

How did your swing thoughts work? _____

_____

strengths from this round: _____

areas to work on: _____

goals for next time: _____

swing thoughts for next time: _____

course: _____ date: ___/___/___ score: _____

Difficulty of Course / Conditions

yardage: _____ tees used: _____ slope: _____ course difficulty: _____

hole locations: _____ course conditions: _____

playing conditions: _____

nature of play: _____ ailments: _____

Performance Ratings

overall round performance: _____ driving: _____ fairway woods: _____

long irons: _____ mid-irons: _____ short irons: _____ wedges: _____

pitching: _____ sand play: _____ chipping: _____ lag putting: _____

short putts: _____ mid-range putts: _____ other: _____

patience: _____ confidence: _____ perseverance: _____ focus: _____

Goals

pre-round goals: _____

pre-round swing thoughts: _____

pre-round short game thoughts: _____

pre-round putting thoughts: _____

pre-round strategy: _____

Key Shots

memorable shots: _____

_____

_____

_____

_____

_____

Close your eyes and visualize good shots that you hit today. Repeat a few times.

shots needing improvement: _____

_____

_____

_____

_____

_____

_____

Visualize yourself in the same situations hitting good shots.

Mental Toughness

Describe good decisions made today, positive emotions, and other mental strengths:

_____

_____

_____

Describe mental mistakes or lapses, but in your mind, focus on the good, not the bad:

_____

_____

_____

Assessment

Which goals did you meet? _____

Which goals were not met? _____

How did your swing thoughts work? _____

_____

strengths from this round: _____

areas to work on: _____

goals for next time: _____

swing thoughts for next time: _____

course: _____ date: ___/___/___ score: _____

Difficulty of Course / Conditions

yardage: _____ tees used: _____ slope: _____ course difficulty: _____

hole locations: _____ course conditions: _____

playing conditions: _____

nature of play: _____ ailments: _____

Performance Ratings

overall round performance: _____ driving: _____ fairway woods: _____

long irons: _____ mid-irons: _____ short irons: _____ wedges: _____

pitching: _____ sand play: _____ chipping: _____ lag putting: _____

short putts: _____ mid-range putts: _____ other: _____

patience: _____ confidence: _____ perseverance: _____ focus: _____

Goals

pre-round goals: _____

pre-round swing thoughts: _____

pre-round short game thoughts: _____

pre-round putting thoughts: _____

pre-round strategy: _____

Key Shots

memorable shots: _____

_____

_____

_____

_____

_____

Close your eyes and visualize good shots that you hit today. Repeat a few times.

shots needing improvement: _____

_____

_____

_____

_____

_____

Visualize yourself in the same situations hitting good shots.

Mental Toughness

Describe good decisions made today, positive emotions, and other mental strengths:

_____

_____

_____

Describe mental mistakes or lapses, but in your mind, focus on the good, not the bad:

_____

_____

_____

Assessment

Which goals did you meet? _____

Which goals were not met? _____

How did your swing thoughts work? _____

_____

strengths from this round: _____

areas to work on: _____

goals for next time: _____

swing thoughts for next time: _____

course: _____ date: ___/___/___ score: _____

Difficulty of Course / Conditions

yardage: _____ tees used: _____ slope: _____ course difficulty: _____

hole locations: _____ course conditions: _____

playing conditions: _____

nature of play: _____ ailments: _____

Performance Ratings

overall round performance: _____ driving: _____ fairway woods: _____

long irons: _____ mid-irons: _____ short irons: _____ wedges: _____

pitching: _____ sand play: _____ chipping: _____ lag putting: _____

short putts: _____ mid-range putts: _____ other: _____

patience: _____ confidence: _____ perseverance: _____ focus: _____

Goals

pre-round goals: _____

pre-round swing thoughts: _____

pre-round short game thoughts: _____

pre-round putting thoughts: _____

pre-round strategy: _____

Key Shots

memorable shots: _____

_____

_____

_____

_____

_____

Close your eyes and visualize good shots that you hit today. Repeat a few times.

shots needing improvement: _____

_____

_____

_____

_____

_____

Visualize yourself in the same situations hitting good shots.

Mental Toughness

Describe good decisions made today, positive emotions, and other mental strengths:

_____

_____

_____

Describe mental mistakes or lapses, but in your mind, focus on the good, not the bad:

_____

_____

_____

Assessment

Which goals did you meet? _____

Which goals were not met? _____

How did your swing thoughts work? _____

_____

strengths from this round: _____

areas to work on: _____

goals for next time: _____

swing thoughts for next time: _____

Printed in Great Britain
by Amazon